W9-CID-294

WILD
GREEN THINGS
IN THE CITY
A Book of Weeds

CURLY DOCK

WILD GREEN THINGS IN THE CITY

A Book of Weeds

BY ANNE OPHELIA DOWDEN

Illustrated by the Author

Thomas Y. Crowell Company   New York

29298

For Ray

Printed in Belgium.
Published simultaneously in the United States of America and Belgium, 1972. Also published simultaneously in Canada by Fitzhenry & Whiteside Limited, Toronto. This work is protected internationally in countries that are members of the Berne Union.

Designed by Sallie Baldwin and Anne Ophelia Dowden
All plants pictured in this book — except enlarged details — are exactly 4/5 natural size.

L.C. Card 72-158687
ISBN 0-690-89067-2

1 2 3 4 5 6 7 8 9 10

FOREWORD

This book was written about the heart of New York City. Other large cities will, of course, differ to a greater or lesser extent: many are not so densely covered with tall buildings and paving; some, particularly in the South and on the West Coast, have a different growing season; some, again on the West Coast and in dry sections of the country, have a different set of plants. But every city has its interesting and beautiful weeds; they all behave in much the same way; and they are all affected by the products of man's living.

The majority of the plants chosen here for comments or illustration can be found throughout the United States—indeed, many of them are common throughout the .world. Regional variations show up in the appended weed lists. The Manhattan list is probably representative of all the eastern half of the United States; the Denver list represents dry areas; the Los Angeles list, the warm Southwest.

The surveys for the western cities were made especially for me by two botanical consultants: Dr. Louis Cutter Wheeler, Professor of Botany, Department of Biological Sciences, University of Southern California in Los Angeles;

and Mr. John R. Keith, Research Botanist, Branch of Regional Geochemistry, United States Geological Survey, Denver, Colorado. I am greatly indebted to them for their careful surveys, for living plant specimens, and for numerous botanical suggestions.

I also extend thanks to Dr. Arthur Cronquist, Senior Curator, New York Botanical Garden, who identified some of my more troublesome Composites; to Dr. P. P. Pirone, Plant Pathologist, New York Botanical Garden, who gave me reference material and advice; to Dr. and Mrs. Gordon Alexander, of Boulder, Colorado, who collected and sent living specimens of several western plants; to Mrs. John P. Meece, Miss La Von Wolverton, and Miss Karen Madsen, who in the early stages of this project collected and sent a sampling of Denver's weeds; to Mr. George Kalmbacher, Taxonomist, Brooklyn Botanic Garden, who spent hours in the herbarium helping sort out the species of all the plants I collected in New York; to Mr. and Mrs. Albert Van Vlack, of Canaan, Conn., who allowed the weeds to grow in their immaculate garden in order to provide specimens for my illustrations; to Miss Edith Todd and Miss Myra Kelley, alert companions on my New York survey trips, who kept an eye on the city weed patches in my absence; to my husband, Raymond B. Dowden, who went with me into the seedier fringes of Manhattan and, as manuscript and drawings took shape, was an unobtrusive but helpful critic, a constant aid and support.

CONTENTS

SHEPHERD'S PURSE

GREEN AGAINST GRAY

The color of life is green, but a city is brown, black, and gray. A big city spreads over the earth a crust of brick and concrete, metal and glass. Thousands or millions of people live and work and play there. Tall apartment houses and office buildings rise above paved streets and sidewalks without much breathing space in between. Only a little green can be seen, and that is found mostly in parks, in gardens, in the backyards of a few houses, and high on the terraces of apartment houses.

But all over the city there are also vacant spaces, empty lots where children play, places where apartments do not rise, where streets do not go, or where buildings have been torn down. These may be the dumping places for bottles, cans, boxes, broken furniture — refuse of many kinds. But here, if you look, you can also find weeds: delightful weeds, unpleasant weeds, most often unseen and ignored weeds. Where did they come from? How do they survive?

Look closely as you walk — at the cracks in the sidewalk; along the gutter's edge; in between buildings; around the edges of parking lots covered with asphalt; in old railroad yards, with rails, rockbeds, and cinder banks; along dock sides, where salt air discourages much greenery. Look everywhere, and you will find wild plants in places so unlikely and so unfriendly to growth that you can only be amazed at the toughness and vigor of the plants that survive in the rubble, in the cluttered "gardens" of their own making.

Untended and despised, these green things are the only friendly sights in some areas. Neglected, run-down places are brightened by a patch of lamb's quarters, a tall clump of ragweed, or a variety of grasses. Barren spots come to life in one season, and if they are left untouched for one, two, or three years, they will become tangled wild gardens. If we look closely enough, we can often identify the most astonishing assortment of wild flowers. And they are beautiful. We will find sunflower, aster, Queen Anne's lace, evening primrose, milkweed: fresh green plants with flowers of pink, yellow, white, blue—a rainbow of colors.

What do we call them—wild flowers or weeds, a joy or a nuisance, loved or unloved? They are the orphan plants of a great city—the neglected, the trampled upon, the underprivileged. But isn't it cheering to see a small but beautiful dandelion fighting its way to sunlight between a brick, a bottle, and a tin can in some dingy vacant lot; or a milkweed shoot breaking through an asphalt driveway by its sheer urge to be alive?

Whenever man ceases to be watchful—if he fails to repair a crack in the sidewalk or to remove a pile of dust in a corner—plants will appear. And if large areas are opened up—as in bombed-out London during World War II—they will soon become gardens of wild flowers. Within two years after the big air raids of 1940-41, dozens of species of wild plants had

moved into the London cellar holes and piles of rubble. In the normal times of the 1970's, over 90 species have been found in New York, over 60 in Denver, over 130 in Los Angeles.

In this book we are not concerned with plants of parks and parkways and gardens. They have mostly been put there by man, and though they may have to struggle to stay alive, they are watched over and encouraged by gardeners and replaced promptly when they die. The weeds which come up among them profit from the watering and cultivating and are, in a sense, pampered too.

Neither are we particularly concerned with plants growing in the strips of vegetation that reach into some cities, like Pittsburgh, along the course of hollows or old railroad cuts or places never built upon. These plants are not pioneers, but old-timers, growing in what is really a leftover bit of the country that has remained untouched as the city spread around it. Though they are not cared for and do have to fight for their lives in city smog, they never had to renew themselves in an area that was once cleared. The ancient fertile topsoil is still there, and so are many of the animals and insects that were part of the original life pattern of the region.

The plants that do interest us are the ones that have somehow made their way into places where, one would think, nothing at all could grow. So let us look at what we find in these truly neglected city lots from April through November in New York, Denver, and Chicago, and all year round in Los Angeles and New Orleans. Since — as we shall learn — the color of life is green, we will be cheered and encouraged when we find how much green there is in this concrete jungle.

APRIL—ROOTS

Early in the spring—in early April in much of the United States—we see the first bits of new growth in our city lots. These tiny sprigs of green bring a thrill of expectation, with their promise that winter is over and a new season is awakening. But they are also delightful in themselves—crisp and delicate, pale and sharp in color, beautiful in shape. They actually sparkle against the soot-blackened earth.

As these baby plants push through the soil, they tell us a great deal about the underground parts from which they rise. Many—the tiniest and most delicate—are new sprouts from seeds that have lain dormant in the earth all winter. Stirred by warmer temperatures and longer days, the seeds have germinated and started to grow. They put out, first, a pair of very small seed leaves, then larger leaves of a different shape, and eventually flowers and seeds. The plants called *annuals* come up like this each year, grow, bloom, make new seeds, and die—all in a single season. It is hard to believe that some of these tiny seedlings will, by fall, have grown taller than our heads.

However, not all the new green shoots we see are so small and delicate. Many grow in sturdy little spikes which show

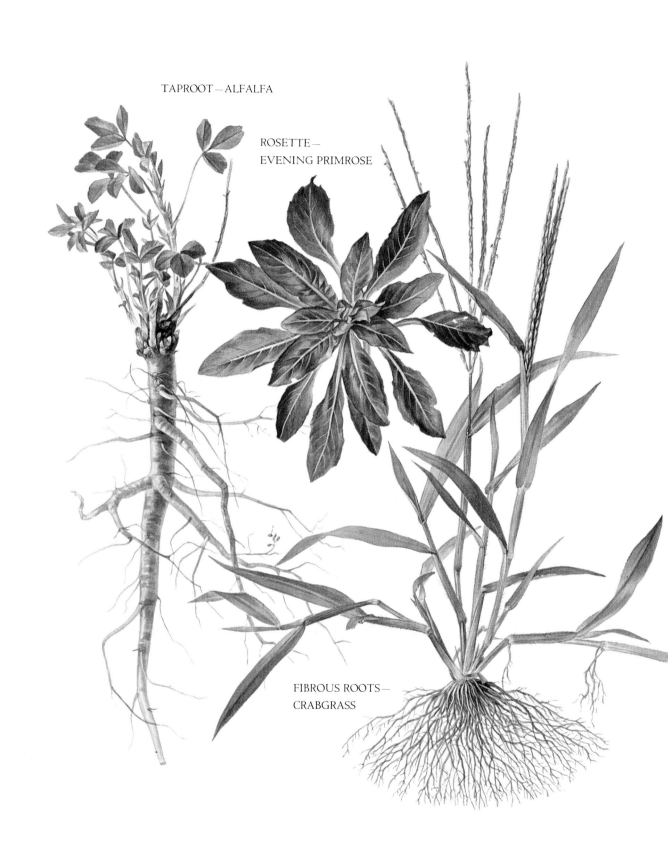

TAPROOT—ALFALFA

ROSETTE—
EVENING PRIMROSE

FIBROUS ROOTS—
CRABGRASS

that they are coming up from a well-established root. These are the *perennials,* with roots that live for many years, sending up every summer a new stalk of leaves and flowers and seeds, which usually dies back in the winter.

And in among the pale new shoots of annuals and perennials, we will also find handsome low-lying rosettes of darker, well-formed leaves. These belong to *biennials,* which in their first summer produced a leafy plant and will bloom in their second growing season. The flat rosettes of some biennials stay green all winter, hugging the earth for warmth and sometimes looking slightly battered by spring. But with the first warm weather, the old leaves lift their tips to the sun and new leaves appear, soon to be followed by a flower stalk. After the flowers have bloomed and formed their seeds, the whole plant will die.

If we pull up any of these different kinds of plants, we will find great variety in their underground parts. The annuals very often have a mass of delicate, threadlike roots. These roots anchor the plant firmly in the earth, and their fine hairs reach out and absorb water from the soil.

This is the first step in a plant's processes of living and growing. In the ground, water forms a film around each tiny soil particle and dissolves some of the minerals in it. Minute root

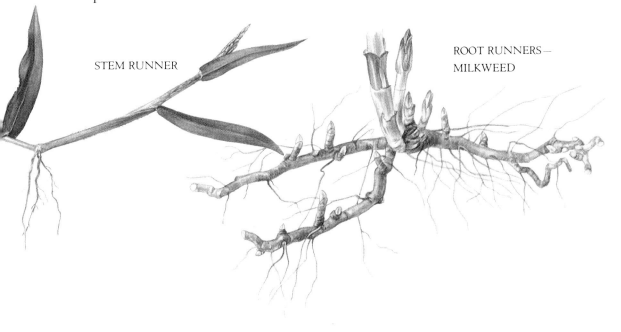

STEM RUNNER

ROOT RUNNERS—
MILKWEED

hairs soak up the water, and the network of small roots carries the solution to the plant stems, which in turn carry it to the leaves. There it will be used in the chemical process that manufactures food for the plant.

Perennials and biennials, of course, also have need of these small rootlets and root hairs. In addition, they need a storage place for food to last through the winter and nourish spring growth before there are leaves to manufacture new food. Most of them have a large main root, or *taproot,* from which the smaller rootlets branch out. In some perennials which live for a long time and grow bigger and bigger each year, these taproots are enormous, and they hold so much nourishment that they send the spring plants up at a surprising rate. The roots of pokeweed are so long and thick that the plant which grows from them in a single summer is as large as a good-sized shrub. Alfalfa roots often reach down 25 feet and have been discovered as deep as 130 feet. Even the fibrous roots of short-lived annuals can grow to amazing length in their search for water. A single four-month-old rye plant (a kind of grass) was found to have roots which, with their root hairs, totaled over 380 *miles* in length. They had an absorbing surface fifty times greater than that of the same plant's stem and leaves.

So it is not always easy to pull up a plant for close inspection. The roots of some weeds form a tangle of underground runners, spreading in all directions and sending up new plants all along their length. Other runners are not roots at all, but stems that travel under the ground or on its surface, rooting and sprouting at the leaf nodes.

All these roots may be more useful than beautiful, but they are very important in the life of a plant.

AILANTHUS

MAY—LEAVES

By early May there is green everywhere in the byways of the city. A few of the smaller plants have reached their full size and are getting ready to bloom. But most are still pushing their stems upward and unfurling more and more leaves. By now we can recognize and identify all the different kinds—the kinds which, as tiny opening plantlets in April, were often hard to tell apart.

And these leafy plants are mostly very beautiful, especially at this time of year, before soot has darkened their bright, fresh green. Some, like yarrow and Queen Anne's lace, have leaves as feathery and delicate as those of any fern. Some, like thistle and dandelion, have jagged leaves with interesting outlines. Some,

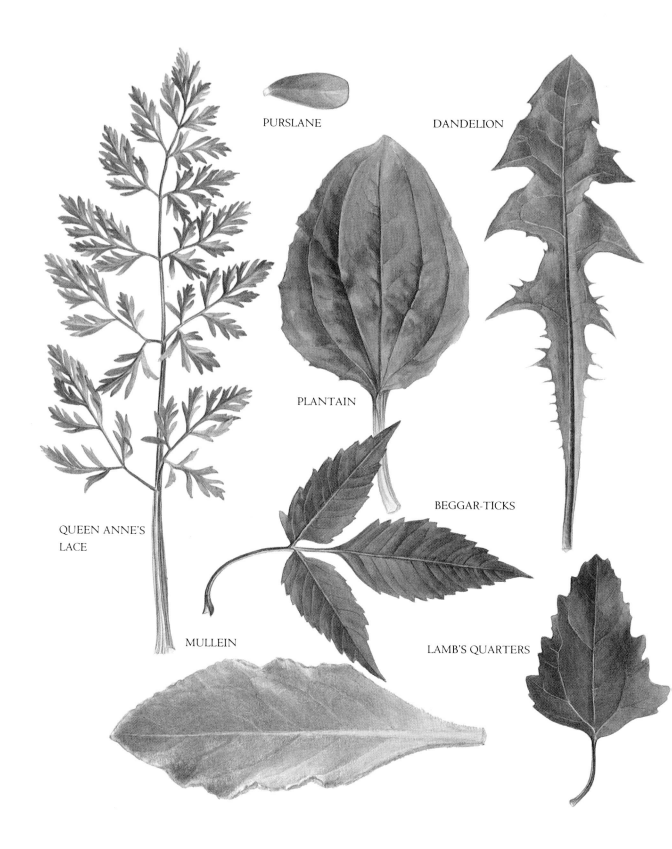

PURSLANE

DANDELION

PLANTAIN

QUEEN ANNE'S
LACE

BEGGAR-TICKS

MULLEIN

LAMB'S QUARTERS

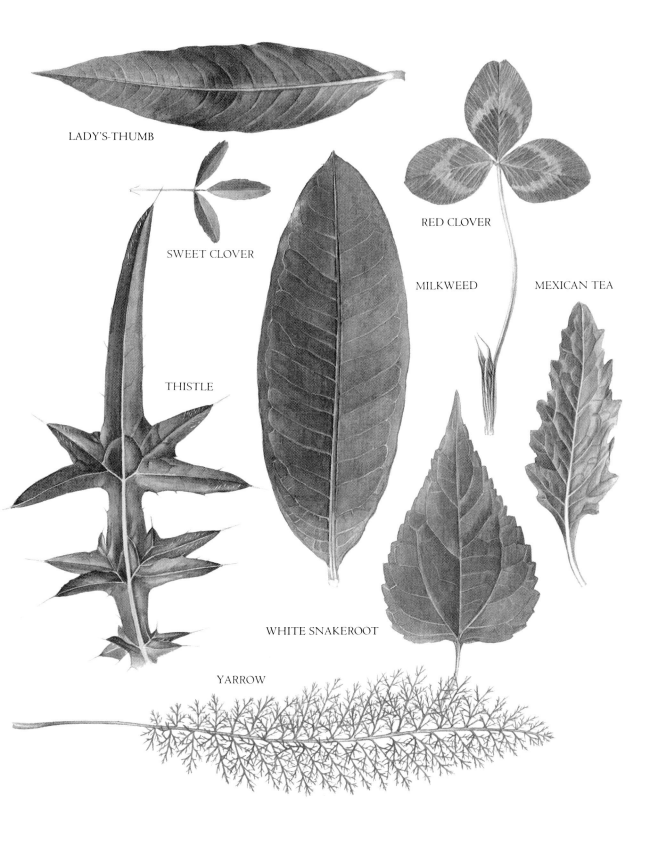

LADY'S-THUMB

SWEET CLOVER

RED CLOVER

MILKWEED

MEXICAN TEA

THISTLE

WHITE SNAKEROOT

YARROW

like mugwort, have leaves dark on top and silvery gray underneath. Mullein's biennial rosette looks as though it were made of soft fuzzy pieces of blanket. Plantain leaves, oval or ribbon-shaped, are striped with prominent straight veins. In some plants, like the various clovers, small leaflets are clustered in groups of three or more.

There is almost endless variety in these leaves, with all their different shapes and textures. But two things they all have in common are green color and a lot of surface to expose to the sun. In fact, the leaves of most plants are very thin; they are practically all surface, and the surfaces always reach out toward the strongest light. This is because of the way a leaf functions in making food for the plant.

In the leaf cells there is water that has come up from the roots, and there is carbon dioxide from the air that has entered through tiny pores in the leaf surface. The green substance in the cells, called *chlorophyll*, absorbs energy from sunlight and uses the energy to split the water into its separate chemical parts. Its hydrogen is joined with the carbon dioxide to form a new chemical combination that results in sugars and starches, or carbohydrates. Some of the carbohydrates are changed into fats and oils; and, with the addition of minerals sent up from the rootlets, others are made into proteins. All these new substances are food for the plants, necessary for growth and for the production of seeds. During the chemical activity in the leaves, unused oxygen and water vapor escape through the pores.

Thus, leaves can be pictured as food factories. Sunlight is the power; chlorophyll is the power transformer; carbon dioxide and water are the raw materials; sugar, starch, protein, and oil are the finished products; and oxygen is a by-product. Since oxygen sustains the life of all breathing creatures, these plants, as they grow, keep the animal world from dying of suffocation. Even the grass on a plot twenty-five feet square gives off enough oxygen to supply a grown person day after day.

The same substances that nourish plants also nourish the animals that eat them. Man, of course, is one of these animals; and, whether he eats the plants themselves or the animals that ate the plants, in the long run he owes his existence to the chemical activity in green leaves. They provide both food and breath of life.

This chemical activity, called *photosynthesis,* takes place all the time in green cells in the presence of light. Chlorophyll ceaselessly creates, harnessing the sun in the production of living matter out of inert gas and water. Here, in these green leaves, is the link between the sun and life on earth.

MUGWORT

INSECT-POLLINATED FLOWERS

EVENING PRIMROSE

SWEET CLOVER

WILD MUSTARD

QUEEN ANNE'S LACE

ALFALFA

FIELD BINDWEED

BUTTER-AND-EGGS

JUNE—FLOWERS

By early June the city is full of blooming wild flowers. Few of them are as large and handsome as the blossoms we find in a garden or a florist's window. But this is reasonable, because cultivated plants, though they once grew wild somewhere in the world, have been carefully selected by man and carefully bred — sometimes for centuries. Many of them could not exist now without the care they receive. So we will not expect our vacant lot to glow like a garden of prize roses. But it does have color enough to tempt us from a distance, and there are dozens of exquisite small blossoms to reward a close-up look.

Later in the season, when tall asters and goldenrods fill both city and country fields with their masses of bloom, the vacant lots do rival a cultivated garden. Early or late, white and yellow are the colors we see most. They predominate here even more than they do in the general floral landscape of the United States, where they are so common that it has been suggested that yellow might well be our national color and goldenrod our national flower.

MULLEIN

MILKWEED

WILD MUSTARD

INSECT-POLLINATED FLOWERS, ENLARGED

Anyone looking at this mass of bloom could never share the curious idea of some people that "weeds do not have flowers." Though there are some plants, like mosses, lichens, and ferns, that have no blossoms, all those in city lots do bear flowers—usually in great profusion. These flowers are a necessary, working part of a plant, like leaves or stems or roots. They are the reproductive organs of the plant—the part that makes the seeds that will carry on the species.

A typical flower has certain basic parts. In its center there is a pistil or a group of pistils, the female part of the blossom.

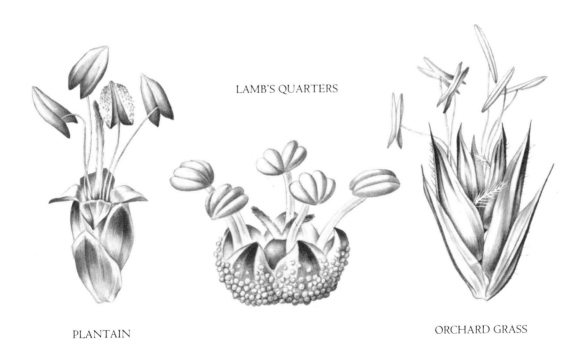

LAMB'S QUARTERS

PLANTAIN

ORCHARD GRASS

WIND-POLLINATED FLOWERS, ENLARGED

Around this is a ring of stamens, the male part. Pistils and stamens are surrounded by petals, and these in turn are encircled by sepals. Most flowering plants, like animals, can produce offspring only after male sperm cells have fertilized female egg cells. In the majority of these plants, each flower bears both male and female cells. The female cells are contained in the ovary at the base of the pistil; the male cells come from the pollen produced by the stamens. Ovary and stamens often grow very close together, and yet as a general rule, the egg cells of a flower are fertilized by sperm cells from another flower of the same kind.

Thus, with only a few exceptions, all blossoms have to be *pollinated* to produce seeds. Pollen from the stamens of a flower on one plant has to reach the pistil of a flower on another plant. Something has to carry the pollen from one flower to another, and in the city this something is most often either the wind or an insect. This basic need for pollination accounts for the size and shape and color of all blossoms everywhere.

Most of the flowers that catch our eye are insect-pollinated. Many have large, bright petals; in other cases, small florets are grouped into large clusters. At any rate, we can see them from a distance, and so can an insect. He will notice a spray of sweet clover and fly to it—not, of course, because he admires its yellow color or beautifully formed petals and not because he enjoys its pleasant fragrance. These things are merely a signal that here is a store of the nectar he wants to eat. As he enters the flower to get the nectar, he is almost always brushed with pollen, which he carries on his body to the next flower he visits. We can always expect colorful flowers, and fragrant ones, to be pollinated by insects.

WIND-POLLINATED FLOWERS

MEXICAN TEA

ENGLISH
PLANTAIN

LAMB'S
QUARTERS

BARNYARD
GRASS

ROUGH
PIGWEED

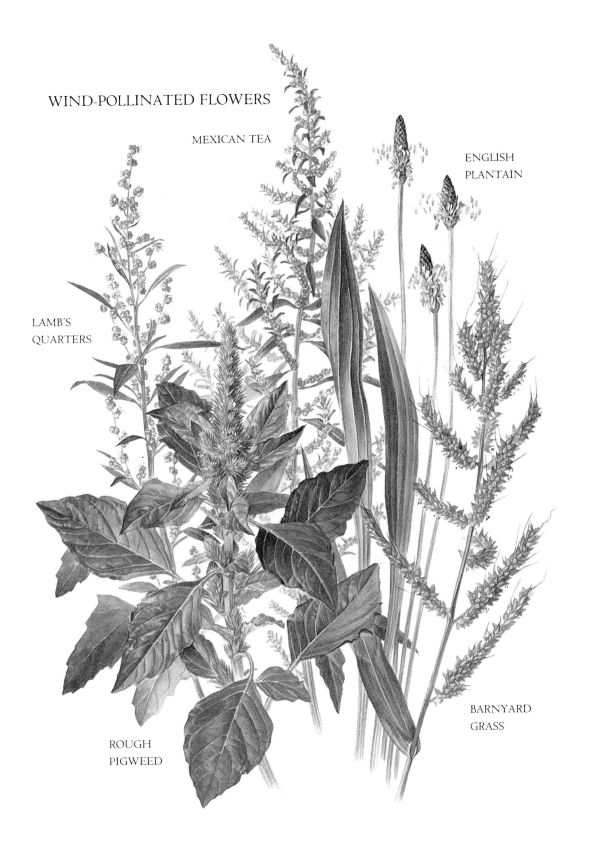

However, a great many of our June plants will not have colorful or fragrant flowers; in fact, they may appear to have no flowers at all. In some cases, like that of the fall-blooming asters, these are still to come; but other plants are already blooming right before our eyes, so inconspicuously that we haven't noticed them. They are wind-pollinated, and we don't recognize the blossoms because they don't look like our idea of what a flower should be.

Wind-pollinated flowers have no need of any of the things that attract insects. They shed clouds of light, dry pollen that is carried in the air at random, so that some of it is bound to reach other flowers of the same species. Bright petals have nothing to do with the pollen's reaching its destination — they would, in fact, actually be in the way. So wind-pollinated flowers have very small petals or none at all. They often look like tiny green buds, and we know that they are blooming only when their yellow stamens project into the breeze to shed pollen and their feathery pistils stand out to catch it. But, examined closely, the tiny florets often prove to be very beautiful.

Practically all grasses are wind-pollinated, and so are plantain, dock, and lamb's quarters — all common in city lots. The flying pollen of some of these flowers, especially that of the much-hated ragweed, is the cause of the hay-fever misery that claims so many victims every summer.

Disk floret   Ray floret

SUNFLOWER

SUMMER—COMPOSITES AND GRASSES

By now a succession of blossoms has come and gone—first the early dandelions, then the docks, the plantains, the clovers, and many others. But some plants still keep us guessing. Though they have tall stalks of vigorous leaves, they are taking their time about blooming. When they do finally show their colors, many of them will prove to be asters, goldenrods, beggarticks—all members of one family, the Composites.

21

BEGGAR-TICKS

SOW THISTLE

CHICORY

GOLDENROD

MUGWORT

BURDOCK

ASTER

GOAT'S BEARD

This is one of the largest and most highly developed of all plant families. It has members that are adapted to a great variety of places and a great variety of conditions. Many of our loveliest wild flowers, like sunflower and chicory, are composites, and also some of our dullest, like ragweed and mugwort.

These flowers are varied and interesting. They are called composites because their heads are composed of dozens — sometimes hundreds — of tiny florets. If we pull apart the big "flower," or *head*, of a sunflower, we will find that its dark central disk is made up of a tightly packed group of very small tubular florets, each with five petals surrounding stamens and pistil. Around the disk is a ring of yellow *rays*, each of which is also a true flower. The florets in the sunflower's disk seem small, but they are large compared to those of a plant like goldenrod. Here the smallest sprig of the flower cluster holds several dozen heads, and each head is made up of a group of disk florets and ray florets. There are thousands on every blooming plant. We can easily pull them apart and see them with the naked eye, but their delicate structure is really clear only when they are examined through a magnifying glass.

This general composite pattern has many variations: dandelions are formed entirely of ray florets; burdocks have only tubular disk florets. Some heads are large and bright so that they attract insects; some are tiny and dull and pollinated by the wind. But all of them profit from this arrangement of closed-packed masses of flowers. One insect in one visit can distribute pollen over dozens of them, or else the wind can pick up their pollen in clouds. Each head produces great numbers of encased seeds, and in most composites these seeds are equipped with excellent devices for distribution. Many have a crown of hairs like the well-known parachutes of the dandelion; others have bristles or are contained in spiny burs. So it is no wonder that the majority of the bright flowers in our city lots belong to this large and thriving family.

However, if we pay attention to less colorful plants, we will find that another big family is just as well represented—the Grasses. Grasses are nearly all wind-pollinated, so they never have showy flowers. But they do have flowers, usually grouped in dense clusters and always very small. In fact, grass flowers are so small that it is almost impossible to tell anything about them without a magnifying glass, which is a pity because some

Male flowers enlarged

Female flowers enlarged

RAGWEED

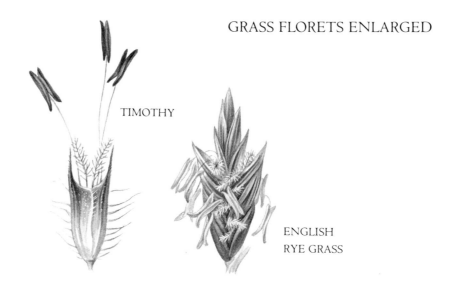

TIMOTHY

ENGLISH
RYE GRASS

of them are very beautiful. But even unmagnified grass plants are worth looking at, with their graceful leaves and stems and feathery clusters of flowers.

It is very easy to overlook this beauty and to take the grass family for granted. We are likely to think of it as the background for other plants—a green carpet in a lawn or a pasture or a prairie. In these places it serves the very important function of keeping the soil from drying up and blowing away or washing away in rain or flood. But it is also useful to man as the source of nearly all his cereals: wheat, rice, corn, and many other grains are the seeds of grasses.

These two enormous plant families, Grasses and Composites, so different in appearance and habit, account for more than half of all the species we will find in our city wild-flower gardens.

26

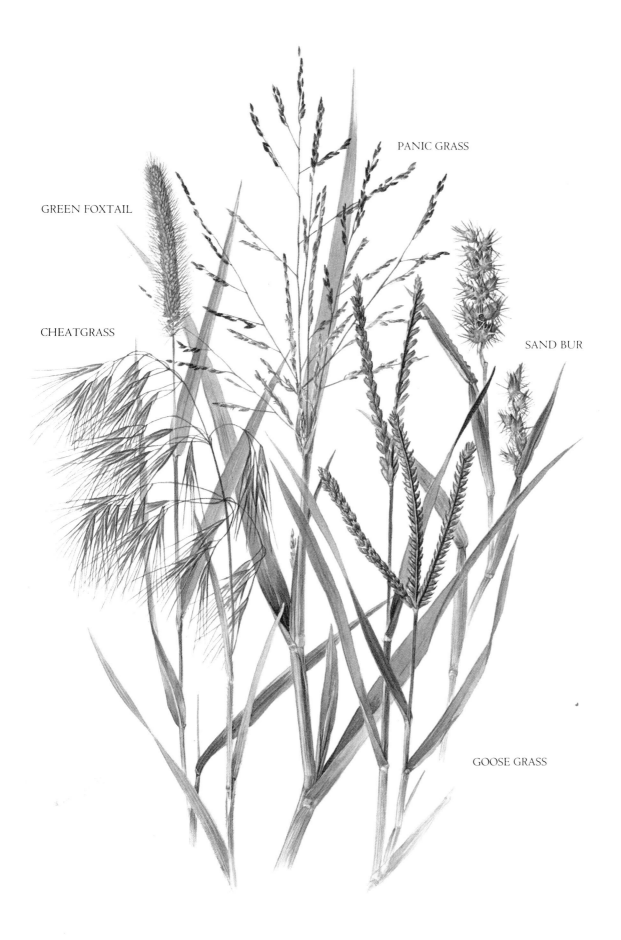

PANIC GRASS

GREEN FOXTAIL

CHEATGRASS

SAND BUR

GOOSE GRASS

WHEAT

AUTUMN — SEEDS

The arrival of fall does not bring an end to our wild flowers. Some, like the asters, are just reaching their peak of bloom; and, since frost comes late in the city, many others will be putting out new blossoms well into November. But in general, autumn is the time for seeds. Annuals and biennials must get theirs ripened and distributed if there are to be any new plants next spring. Perennials also prepare for their winter sleep with new seeds, as well as with well-stocked roots.

So now the vacant lots are full of fruiting plants, bearing their seeds in a great variety of interesting and handsome containers. Here is the material for all kinds of dry winter bouquets. Tall stalks of evening primrose are covered with pods like little fluted vases that open at the top to spill out their seeds. Milkweed's graceful pointed pods split down the side and release masses of chocolate-brown seeds with silky white parachutes. Dock has spikes of rich brown seeds that look like coffee grounds from a distance, but prove on examination to be three-angled and delicately winged. The flat flower clusters of

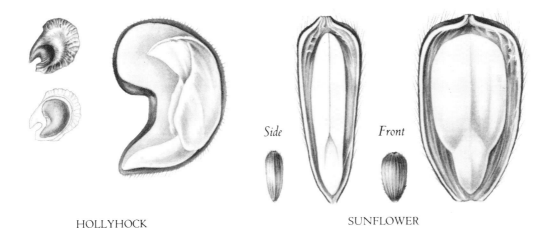

HOLLYHOCK   *Side*   *Front*   SUNFLOWER

Queen Anne's lace have curled up to form lacy gray tangles like birds' nests, holding masses of strange prickly seeds. The fruiting sprays of grasses have many beautiful shapes, some nodding and feathery, some stiff and upright, often with spreading bristles.

Some of these "seeds," because their structure includes more than the simple seed, should be called schizocarps, achenes, samaras, etc. But for all practical purposes they are the same as ordinary seeds, and that is what we will call them here.

Whatever form they take, all seeds are basically tiny new plants packed in containers that will keep them safe until time for them to start to grow. Often the baby plants, or *embryos,* are so minute that they occupy only part of the space in even the smallest seeds. The rest is filled with food—starch and protein for nourishment when growing starts. Sometimes, as in the sunflower, the inside of the seed is filled by the plump baby plant, which has already absorbed all the food. This same food is an important part of the diet of animals and men. We

29

CURLY DOCK

EVENING PRIMROSE

ASTER

QUEEN ANNE'S
LACE

SUNFLOWER

PEPPERGRASS

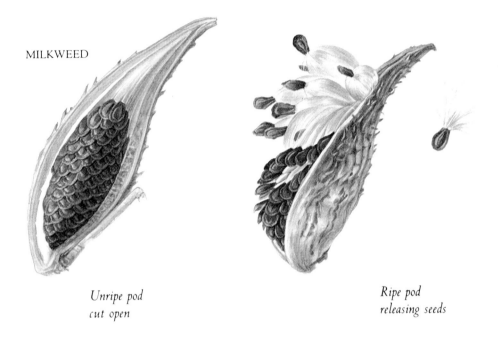

MILKWEED

Unripe pod
cut open

Ripe pod
releasing seeds

eat seeds in the form of beans, nuts, and grains or cereals; and we also put their starches, proteins, and oils to uses as varied as the manufacture of paints and the making of plastics.

Once ripened, some seeds must quickly find a place to grow or they will die. But most seeds require a resting period, which usually means a period of waiting for conditions that will favor the young plant when it begins to grow. Enclosed in a protective coat, often extremely hard and waterproof, embryos and food dry out and pass into a dormant or sleeping state. They appear to be dead. Indeed, their life processes slow down so that they can not be measured by any known method, and in this state the seed awaits the proper time for awakening and growth. Some seeds can wait a very long time. There are reliable records of seeds kept in dry storage that were able to grow after 158 years, and somewhat questionable reports of seeds still alive after a thousand years. These, of course, are rare instances. Most fancy garden seeds can last only a year or two. But the seeds of some of our wild plants are known to have lain buried in the earth for ten, forty, and even eighty years, after which they were still able to germinate and produce healthy plants.

The conditions that cause a seed to awake, or germinate, are many and complex. Oxygen and warmth play a part, but the most important awakener is water. In places where there is no cold winter, it is the rainy season that stirs the plant world to growth. A seed drinks in water and starts to swell, and soon the embryo begins to lengthen. Even at this early stage, its cells bear the character of their future functions. Some grow unerringly up toward the air, to become stems and leaves; others grow downward to become roots; and our yearly cycle is ready to begin again.

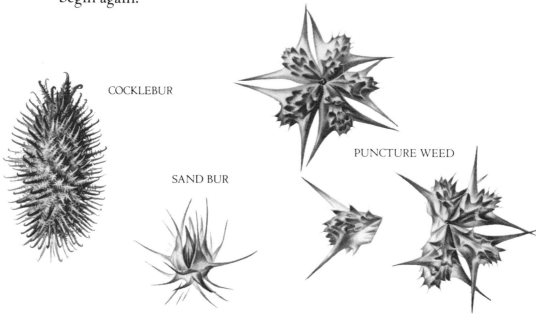

COCKLEBUR

SAND BUR

PUNCTURE WEED

SEEDS AND SEED CONTAINERS, ENLARGED

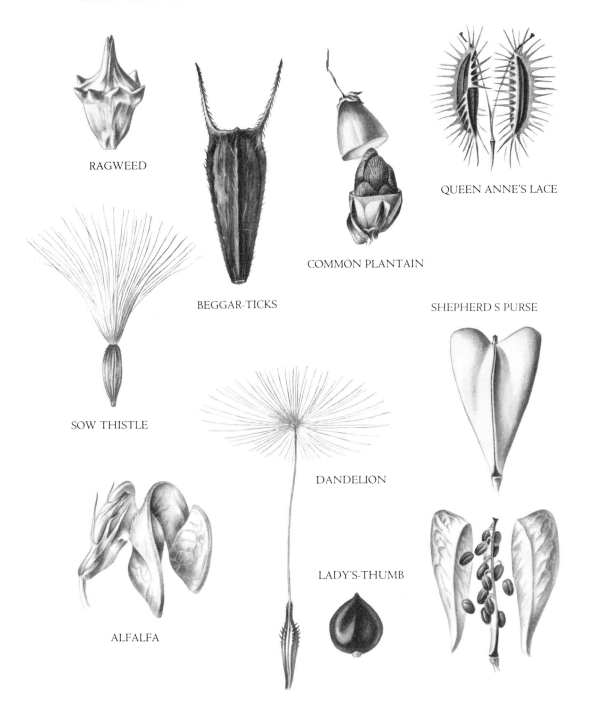

RAGWEED

BEGGAR-TICKS

COMMON PLANTAIN

QUEEN ANNE'S LACE

SOW THISTLE

SHEPHERD S PURSE

DANDELION

ALFALFA

LADY'S-THUMB

SURVIVAL

After discovering all this about the way plants grow and what they need for life, we wonder more than ever how it is possible for our vacant-lot gardens to exist. How do the plants get there in the first place? How do they manage to survive in seemingly impossible situations? These are really tremendous questions, but city dwellers generally take them for granted, when they notice the wild plants at all. People who may be trying desperately to keep a shrub alive or make a houseplant bloom in the adverse conditions of the city seldom stop to think that the success of the uncared-for wild things is almost miraculous.

In the vacant spot left by a torn-down city building, there are usually no living seeds in the newly bared earth. The place may be separated from other green areas by several blocks of tall buildings and paved streets. And yet the wild seeds quickly arrive. They root and grow in a place that would seem to lack even the most basic necessities for life.

In nature, the vegetation of any area is the result of many factors working together — soil, air, rain, light, temperature, animal life. The soil must contain the water and minerals necessary for the manufacture of food. It must be loose enough that water and air and roots can penetrate it. It is normally fertilized by creatures that eat and digest plant material and return its minerals to the soil in excretion and in death. It must contain the bacteria, molds, and other fungi that break down dead animal and plant organisms into their original components, for the green plants to use again in a new cycle.

And yet our city wild flowers grow in earth that is packed hard, with few spaces for the vital water film to collect around soil particles. Few earthworms tunnel to loosen the soil. It is "fertilized" by the discarded products of city life rather than the discarded bodies of living things. Rainwater falling on the hard-packed surface is likely to run off too quickly to penetrate to root level, or else it stands in badly drained puddles and threatens to drown the roots. The plants live in a constant fall of soot. This and the oily black film that coats the leaves and smudges our hands when we pick a bouquet damage the plant by clogging some of its tiny breathing pores and by cutting down the sunlight that reaches the chlorophyll. In fact, the heavy canopy of smog that hangs over many cities has already shut out a good portion of the natural sunlight. The air is full of poisonous chemicals poured out by car motors, incinerators, and factory chimneys—poisons that burn the leaves and break down their chlorophyll. Some of them also make the soil so acid that they kill the bacteria and fungi that normally act on dead matter.

And in the canyons of the city, many of the insects that pollinate wild flowers are missing. Honeybees and bumblebees are by far the most important pollinators in the country, but they rarely venture into the cement-and-brick parts of our cities. They are found only in the more open lots and in parks and botanic gardens, where they often live in hives specially provided by man.

Most plants can not live at all under these conditions, so our city weeds certainly do not have to fight for growing space. But they do have to fight for almost everything else, and it is important to find out what traits give some plants the ability to do so well in spite of so many difficulties. In the first place, how did they arrive? A growing plant, of course, spends its life where it is rooted, but its seeds can make their way out into the world for long distances. This is the reason for all the parachutes and wings and barbs that we have found on so many city seeds. The flying seeds of milkweed, dandelion, goldenrod, and ailanthus are carried on the wind by the thousands—even by the millions. They lodge in all kinds of places, and many of them can germinate and grow in the most unlikely spots—in the chink of a brick wall or in a small handful of dust in the corner of a roof— as well as in any earth man opens up for them.

Seeds equipped with spines, like those of beggar-ticks, or enclosed in bristly pods, like those of burdock, catch in the hair of animals or the clothing of people and hitch a ride to a new home. The small seeds of some plants, like peppergrass, are provided with a glue which, when moistened by dew, can fasten them to the feet of birds. Some plants—the tumbleweeds of the West—which evolved in dry open country, break from their roots when they have reached maturity. The whole plant rolls along before the wind, scattering seeds as it goes. Sometimes these plants can be found growing near Eastern railroad yards, carried thousands of miles from home on the wheels of trains.

Many seeds are not especially equipped for travel. They drop directly down at the roots of their parent plant and soon increase the population in that particular spot. But they also, of course, manage to get to new places, carried perhaps in the mud on a pigeon's feet or in his gizzard. Many seeds can be eaten by birds and pass unharmed through their digestive systems, to be dropped eventually at some distant place.

Once settled in a new location, many of our wild flowers can produce hundreds of new plants without seeds. In some species,

like thistle, milkweed, and toadflax, the roots send out runners from which new plantlets sprout. In others, stems may lie flat on the ground or travel underground, root at the leaf nodes, and send up a new plant at each node. This is true of mugwort, yarrow, and many grasses. Once a plant of this sort becomes established, it will soon be the center of a colony that grows ever denser as the years pass.

Most of the plants that thrive in a city lot are the ones that even in the country do not need a fertile soil. There are, of course, some useful materials in city earth. Its minerals are renewed to a certain extent by the plants that die each year, fall to the ground, and decay there. Members of the pea family — clover, melilot, alfalfa—are especially valuable to the plant community because their roots are able to capture a rich store of nitrogen that is returned to the soil at their death. And a few animal bodies also return their minerals to the earth—a rat, a stray cat, a bird, many kinds of insects.

All this may explain the plants' ability to survive, but their pollination still presents us with questions. Part of the answer is found in the fact that a great number of our city plants are wind-pollinated. These include the grasses, ragweed, lamb's quarters, wormseed, dock, and the plaintains—all of which grow in great profusion.

But the many insect-pollinated flowers are another matter. Evening primrose should be pollinated by night-flying moths. Other plants, like milkweed, burdock, and red clover, would in the country be pollinated by bees or butterflies; and they have had to find other pollinators in places where no bees come at all. There are a few butterflies, even in the heart of the city— occasionally a surprising and beautiful flock of migrating monarchs. And great numbers of wasps and flies of all kinds are everywhere. These presumably transfer the pollen, though they often seem to be the wrong size and shape for the job. There are also a few beetles, but, at best, beetles are poor pollinators, and they usually eat the flowers and are enemies rather than friends.

However, many of these flowers can pollinate themselves when other means fail, and some species, including a large number of our weeds, do this habitually. There are even some plants, like the dandelion, that can produce seeds without any pollination at all.

Whatever the method, the plants do get pollinated, and many of them produce seeds in enormous numbers. A large tumbling pigweed was found to have more than six million seeds to shed as it rolled before the wind. This is one of the secrets of the success of weeds. A great number of seeds, well equipped to travel and to survive, may be more important than the toughness of the plant itself.

DANDELION

THE WAYS OF WEEDS

In the eyes of many people, our city wild flowers are just weeds. This makes us wonder, What is a weed? It is not necessarily an unattractive plant. A dandelion is as beautiful as a chrysanthemum and would be as highly valued if it did not grow by the millions in green lawns where it is not wanted. Actually, this gives us the answer to our question: a weed is any plant that grows where man doesn't want it to. Some of the most beautiful wild flowers of country roadsides are considered weeds if they come up in a farmer's wheatfield or in someone's rose garden. When they appear in dreary spots in the middle of a city, they again become precious and worthy of admiration.

There are, however, certain qualities that make plants "weedy." They are the qualities that we have found in our city plants—vigor, ability to travel, ability to reproduce themselves under all kinds of conditions. These traits were acquired by the ancestors of our weeds long ago and often far away. The majority of our weeds came to America from foreign lands. Most came from Europe, carried here intentionally or accidentally by the earliest settlers and by later generations of traders. The ones that landed on the East Coast came to a country that was covered with dense forests and a balance of wild life that had existed for millions of years. When trees were cut down and large areas cleared for farming, the sun-loving, open-field plants from Europe found an ideal place in which to spread. They had little competition from native American plants of the region, which were more at home in the moist shade of the woods.

Many plants that began to run wild had been cherished flowers or vegetables in Old World gardens. The settlers brought with them seeds or rooted pieces of the plants they were accustomed to grow for ornament and food and medicine. Many of these now grow wild in the United States, and some—like mustard, mugwort, and toadflax—are vigorous enough to make their way into city lots. Clovers and grasses were brought for grazing cows and horses. And dozens of plants which were despied as weeds even in their homeland traveled here unseen in bales of hay, in packing materials, in the earth that was often used as ballast for ships.

The very first immigrant plants were brought to the West Coast by the Spaniards, and many of them are now common

SOME WESTERN WEEDS

RUSSIAN THISTLE

OX-TONGUE

BUFFALO-BUR

PUNCTURE
WEED

weeds in California. A few have reached the United States in recent years from Asia and the Southern Hemisphere, but the greatest number of new plants landed long ago on the East Coast. These have been making their way westward ever since, settling down wherever soil and temperature and rainfall make life possible for them. They become weeds wherever the native population of plants is not strong enough to crowd them out. Man has made this migration possible. He has moved westward, cutting down forests, ploughing fields, building roads, changing natural drainage—thus opening up new homes for new plants. He has also furnished transportation for them, often without knowing it.

Some of our weeds, of course, are native Americans—plants originally limited to small open areas and now given new opportunities by the changed countryside. These include some of the handsomest ones found in city lots: sunflower, goldenrod, aster, milkweed. And there has also been a certain amount of west-to-east migration, as some plants of the western plains, like ragweed, have spread rapidly in the East.

BLACK BINDWEED

PURSLANE

PLANTS AND PEOPLE

For more than a million years, plants and human beings have lived together on earth. From the beginning, they were both part of the "web of life," the beautifully balanced natural pattern in which all living things depend on one another. Only after man became civilized did he begin to feel that plants were to be grown for his food, shelter, and pleasure or else to be removed or avoided.

The first steps toward civilization were taken when Stone Age man discovered that he could cultivate the seeds, fruits, and roots he liked to eat, instead of gathering them only where he found them growing wild. When he became a farmer, he settled down and began to change his environment. Since then—for

thousands of years—man has been cutting forests, clearing fields, draining swamps, building cities, but at the same time caring for and encouraging much of the green world around him.

Of course, his life depended on that green world. As we have seen, there would be no life on earth without chlorophyll: it harnesses the sun's energy and starts the chemical processes that convert minerals and gases into the materials that make up the bodies of plants and animals. All the oxygen we breathe is produced by plants. All our food comes, directly or indirectly, from plants. They provide clothing and shelter, as well as medicine for our physical ills and balm for our spirits.

We still depend on the green world, and yet we are steadily destroying it. There is now hardly a place on earth that man has not touched in some way. And in the places where he has been established for a long time, his cities are spreading in all directions, swallowing up the wild spaces. Our precious green areas are shrinking away. Even the farms and orchards and pasturelands are disappearing. While the human population is growing, the plant population is decreasing; and if this dislocation of nature's balance goes much further, the plants will eventually be unable to support the people.

Even worse for plants than the loss of growing space is the devastation caused by the poisonous materials that now pollute air, water, and earth. Every city has a canopy of smog—a hanging cloud of soot, oil, carbon monoxide, sulfur dioxide, or ozone—bad for the breathing processes of both plants and people. These smogs are spreading out from their urban centers, killing plants miles away. In the area surrounding Ontario, Canada, smelter fumes have damaged aspen foliage nearly seventy miles distant. Pine trees in the mountains sixty miles from Los Angeles are being killed, apparently by that city's drifting smog.

Factories all over the country are sending clouds of poisonous smoke into the air and masses of poisonous chemical waste into the rivers. Sometimes these poisons kill plants quickly and directly. Sometimes they kill the pollinating insects or the birds, fish, or other animals that are necessary for a balance of nature. Sometimes temperatures of air or water are so changed that they destroy both plants and animals. Tender plants are already dying out in many places, and eventually even our toughest weeds will no longer be able to survive.

It is a terrifying prospect—that a world which has been evolving for more than three hundred million years may be destroyed in one or two generations. But destruction is not inevitable. If we will clean up the air and water, and do it soon enough, the plants will survive. We have seen the remarkable vigor of our city weeds, and in the country we find over and over again examples of nature's wonderful power to renew herself. The plants will take care of themselves if we give them half a chance. All they need is space, clean air, clean water, and clean soil; with these, both the country and the city can be green.

WHITE CLOVER

COMMON
KNOTWEED

LISTS OF WILD PLANTS FOUND IN NEW YORK, DENVER, LOS ANGELES

These lists of plants that grow wild in three United States cities do not pretend to be definitive, but they offer a fair sampling of inner-city weeds.

MANHATTAN   Weeds growing in parking lots, old building sites, railyards, etc.
Collected by Anne Ophelia Dowden

Very Common

Ailanthus altissima: tree of heaven
Ambrosia artemisiifolia: common ragweed, Roman wormwood
Ambrosia trifida: giant ragweed
Artemisia annua: wormwood
Artemisia vulgaris: common mugwort
Aster novi-belgii: New York aster
Aster pilosus: white-heath aster

Bidens frondosa: beggar-ticks, sticktight

Chenopodium album: lamb's quarters, white goosefoot
Chenopodium ambrosioides: Mexican tea, wormseed
Conyza canadensis: horseweed
Digitaria sanguinalis: crab grass
Eleusine indica: yard grass, goose grass
Eupatorium rugosum: white snakeroot
Lactuca scariola (L. serriola): prickly lettuce

Oenothera biennis: evening primrose
Panicum dichotomiflorum: panic grass
Plantago major: common plantain
Plantago rugelii: plantain
Poa pratensis: Kentucky blue-grass
Polygonum aviculare: common knotweed
Polygonum persicaria: lady's-thumb
Setaria viridis: green foxtail
Taraxacum officinale: dandelion

Common

Achillea millefolium: yarrow
Amaranthus graecizans: prostrate amaranth, prostrate pigweed
Apocynum cannabinum: Indian hemp
Arctium minus: burdock
Asclepias syriaca: common milkweed
Bassia hyssopifolia: bassia
Bidens bipinnata: Spanish-needles
Brassica kaber: charlock, wild mustard
Capsella bursa-pastoris: shepherd's purse
Cirsium vulgare: bull thistle, common thistle
Daucus carota: Queen Anne's lace, wild carrot
Echinochloa crusgalli: barnyard grass

Erechtites hieracifolia: pilewort, fireweed
Helianthus annuus: common sunflower
Hieracium pratense: yellow hawkweed, king devil
Lepidium virginicum: peppergrass
Linaria vulgaris: butter-and-eggs, toadflax
Lolium perenne: English rye grass
Medicago sativa: alfalfa
Melilotus alba: white sweet clover
Melilotus officinalis: yellow sweet clover
Panicum capillare: witch grass, panic grass
Phragmites communis: common reed

Plantago lanceolata: English plantain
Polygonum convolvulus: black bindweed
Rumex crispus: curly dock, sour dock
Solanum dulcamara: climbing nightshade, bittersweet
Solanum nigrum: black nightshade
Solidago canadensis: goldenrod
Sonchus oleraceus: common sow thistle
Tragopogon pratensis: goat's beard
Trifolium pratense: red clover
Trifolium procumbens: hop clover
Trifolium repens: white clover
Verbascum thapsus: common mullein, flannel-plant
Xanthium strumarium: cocklebur, clotbur

Rare

Amaranthus retroflexus: rough pigweed, green amaranth
Aster cordifolius: heart-leaved aster

Aster novae-angliae: New England aster
Bromus tectorum: cheatgrass, downy

brome grass
Cichorium intybus: chicory
Convolvulus arvensis: field bindweed

MANHATTAN

Rare (continued)

Cyperus esculentus: yellow nut-grass, chufa

Dactylis glomerata: orchard grass

Equisetum arvense: common horsetail

Eragrostis megastachya: stink-grass

Galinsoga ciliata: galinsoga

Ipomoea purpurea: purple morning glory

Lycopersicon esculentum: tomato

Matricaria matricarioides: pineapple weed

Mollugo verticillata: carpetweed

Papaver somniferum: opium poppy

Phleum pratense: timothy

Phytolacca americana: pokeweed, scoke

Polygonum cuspidatum: Japanese knotweed

Potentilla recta: cinquefoil, five-finger

Rhus glabra: smooth sumac

Rhus radicans: poison ivy

Salsola kali: Russian thistle

Saponaria officinalis: soapwort, bouncing Bet

Silene cucubalus: bladder campion

Solidago graminifolia: grass-leaved goldenrod

Solidago sempervirens: seaside goldenrod

Sonchus uliginosus: sow thistle

Sorghum vulgare: sorghum

Triticum aestivum: wheat

Tussilago farfara: coltsfoot

DENVER   Weeds growing in waste places without irrigation.
Collected by John R. Keith

Very common

Amaranthus gracizans (A. blitoides): prostrate amaranth, prostrate pigweed

Artemisia ludoviciana: prairie sage

Bromus tectorum: cheatgrass, downy brome grass

Chrysothamnus nauseosus: rabbit-brush

Conium maculatum: poison hemlock

Convolvulus arvensis: field bindweed

Conyza canadensis: horseweed

Digitaria sanguinalis: crab grass

Echinochloa crusgalli: barnyard grass

Euphorbia serpyllifolia: thyme-leaved spurge

Kochia iranica: burning-bush

Polygonum aviculare: common knotweed

Portulaca oleracea: purslane

Salsola kali: Russian thistle

Taraxacum officinale: dandelion

Tragopogon dubius: oyster-plant, goat's beard

Tribulus terrestris: puncture weed

Common

Amaranthus retroflexus: rough pigweed, green amaranth

Ambrosia artemisiifolia: common ragweed, Roman wormwood

Ambrosia trifida: giant ragweed

Asclepias speciosa: showy milkweed

Aster laevis: aster

Bassia hyssopifolia: bassia

Capsella bursa-pastoris: shepherd's purse

Cenchrus pauciflorus: sand bur

Chenopodium album: lamb's quarters, white goosefoot

Chenopodium fremontii: goosefoot

Chenopodium rubrum: red goosefoot

Cicuta douglasii: water-hemlock

Croton texensis: croton

Eragrostis diffusa: spreading love-grass

Geranium bicknellii: wild geranium

Grindelia squarrosa: gumweed

Gutierrezia sarothae: snakeweed

Helianthus annuus: common sunflower

Iva xanthifolia: marsh elder

Lactuca scariola (L. serriola): prickly lettuce

Lepidium campestre: peppergrass

Medicago sativa: alfalfa

Melilotus alba: white sweet clover

Melilotus officinalis: yellow sweet clover

Panicum capillare: witch grass, panic grass

Plantago lanceolata: English plantain

Plantago major: common plantain

Polygonum ramosissimum: bushy knotweed

Rumex acetosella: sheep sorrel, dock

Rumex crispus: curly dock, sour dock

Salsola collina: Russian thistle

Saponaria officinalis: soapwort, bouncing Bet

Scirpus lacustris: great bulrush

Solanum rostratum: buffalo-bur

Thlaspi arvense: penny-cress

Typha latifolia: broad-leaved cat-tail

Verbena bracteata: vervain

Arctium minus: burdock
Brassica rapa: bird's rape
Buchloe dactyloides: buffalo grass
Cleome serrulata: Rocky Mountain

bee plant
Daucus carota: Queen Anne's lace, wild carrot
Galinsoga parviflora: galinsoga

Gaura parviflora: gaura
Haplopappus macronema: haplopappus
Mirabilis multiflora: wild four-o'clock
Oxalis stricta: sour-grass

LOS ANGELES   Weeds growing in waste places without irrigation.

Collected by Louis Cutter Wheeler

Very common

Amaranthus albus: tumbleweed
Avena fatua: wild oat
Brassica geniculata: Mediterranean mustard
Chenopodium berlandieri: goosefoot
Conyza bonariensis: South American conyza

Cotula australis: Australian cotula
Cynodon dactylon: Bermuda grass
Erodium cicutarium: red-stemmed filaree
Euphorbia supina: spotted spurge
Hordeum glaucum: wild barley
Lolium multiflorum: Italian rye-grass

Malva parviflora: cheese-weed
Nicotiana glauca: tree tobacco
Picris echioides: bristly ox-tongue
Poa annua: annual blue-grass
Polygonum arenastrum: knotweed
Salsola kali (S. pestifer): Russian thistle
Tribulus terrestris: puncture weed

Common

Amaranthus deflexus: low amaranth
Amaranthus graecizans (A. blitoides): prostrate amaranth, prostrate pigweed
Ambrosia psilostachya: common ragweed
Atriplex semibaccata: Australian saltbush
Bassia hyssopifolia: bassia
Brassica nigra: black mustard
Bromus diandrus: ripgut-grass
Bromus mollis: brome grass
Bromus rubens: foxtail brome grass
Bromus wildenovii: rescue grass
Capsella bursa-pastoris: shepherd's purse
Centaurea melitensis: Napa thistle
Chenopodium album: lamb's quarters, white goosefoot
Chenopodium ambrosioides: Mexican tea, wormseed

Chenopodium murale: wall goosefoot
Cichorium intybus: chicory
Convolvulus arvensis: field bindweed
Conyza canadensis: horseweed
Coronopus didymus: lesser wart-grass
Erodium moschatum: white-stemmed filaree
Foeniculum vulgare: sweet fennel
Franseria acanthicarpa: annual burweed
Helianthus annuus: common sunflower
Heterotheca grandiflora: telegraph weed
Lactuca scariola (L. serriola): prickly lettuce
Malacothrix saxatilis: cliff malacothrix
Matricaria matricarioides: pineapple weed
Medicago hispida: bur-clover
Medicago lupulina: black medic
Oxalis corniculata: creeping woodsorrel

Polycarpon tetraphyllum: four-leaved polycarp
Polygonum aviculare: common knotweed
Raphanus sativus: wild radish
Ricinus communis: castor bean
Roubieva multifida: cut-leaved goosefoot
Rumex crispus: curly dock, sour dock
Setaria geniculata: perennial foxtail
Sisymbrium irio: desert mustard
Sisymbrium orientale: Oriental sisymbrium
Sonchus oleraceus: common sow thistle
Sorghum halepense: Johnson grass
Stellaria media: common chickweed
Stephanomeria virgata: virgate stephanomeria
Taraxacum officinale: dandelion

Rare

Ailanthus altissima: tree of heaven
Amaranthus retroflexus: rough pigweed, green amaranth

Andropogon saccharoides: plumed beardgrass
Anthemis cotula: mayweed

Apium leptophyllum: marsh-parsley
Artemisia californica: coast sagebrush
Artemisia douglasiana: Douglas' mug-

Rare (continued)

wort

Asclepias fascicularis: narrow-leaved milkweed

Atriplex hastata: halberd-leaved orache

Atriplex serenana: bracted saltbush

Avena barbata: slender wild oat

Baccharis emoryi: Emory baccharis

Baccharis pilularis: chaparral broom

Baccharis viminea: mule fat

Beta vulgaris: common beet

Bidens pilosa: beggar-ticks

Brassica hirta: white mustard

Brassica napus: rape

Brickellia californica: California brickellia

Chrysanthemum coronarium: garland chrysanthemum

Chrysothamnus nauseosus: rabbit-brush

Cortaderia sellowiana: pampas grass

Cressa truxillensis: cressa

Datura wrightii: thorn apple

Digitaria sanguinalis: crab grass

Diplotaxis muralis: sand rocket

Distichlis spicata: salt grass

Echinochloa crusgalli: barnyard grass

Emex spinosa: spiny emex

Eremocarpus setigerus: Turkey mullein

Erodium botrys: long-beaked filaree

Euphorbia albomarginata: rattlesnake weed

Euphorbia serpyllifolia: thyme-leaved spurge

Festuca myuros: rattail fescue

Gnaphalium purpureum: purple cudweed

Haplopappus venetus: coastal isocoma

Heliotropium curassavicum: seaside heliotrope

Hypochaeris glabra: smooth cat's-ear

Ipomoea purpurea: purple morning glory

Lepidium oblongum: wayside peppergrass

Lippia nodiflora: garden lippia

Lobularia maritima: sweet alyssum

Lycopersicon esculentum: tomato

Malva neglecta: round-leaved mallow

Marrubium vulgare: common hoarhound

Matthiola incana: stock

Medicago apiculata: smooth-burred medic

Medicago sativa: alfalfa

Melilotus indica: Indian melilot

Mesembryanthemum crystallinum: common ice-plant

Mesembryanthemum edule: Hottentot fig

Mesembryanthemum nodiflorum: slender-leaved ice-plant

Modiola caroliniana: wheel mallow

Oenothera leptocarpa: mustard-like primrose

Oryzopsis miliacea: millet mountain-rice

Parapholis incurvus: sickle grass

Pennisetum clandestinum: kikuyu grass

Phalaris minor: Mediterranean canary grass

Plantago lanceolata: English plantain

Plantago major: common plantain

Polygonum argyrocoleon: silver-sheathed knotweed

Portulaca oleracea: purslane

Prunus armeniaca: apricot

Salix lasiolepis: arroyo willow

Sambucus mexicana: Southwestern elderberry

Senecio mikanioides: German ivy

Sida hederacea: alkali mallow

Silene gallica. common catchfly

Sorghum vulgare: sorghum

Spergularia marina: salt-marsh sand spurry

Spergularia rubra: purple sand spurry

Tetragonia tetragonioides: New Zealand spinach

Trifolium ciliatum: tree clover

Ulmus parvifolia: Chinese elm

Washingtonia robusta: Mexican fan palm

INDEX

(Page numbers in italic refer to illustrations)

ABOUT ANNE OPHELIA DOWDEN

In preparation for this book Anne Ophelia Dowden prowled the streets of Manhattan, watching the progress of city weeds in warehouse areas, parking lots, and the edges of railroad yards.

Mrs. Dowden is recognized as one of America's foremost botanical illustrators. Her work has been exhibited in many museums and galleries and has been published in major magazines throughout the country.

As a child in Colorado, she began her lifelong hobby of collecting and drawing specimens of native plants and insects, a hobby to which she now devotes her full time. She received a B.A. in art from the Carnegie Institute of Technology in Pittsburgh, and after graduation continued her studies in New York, where she has lived ever since. She has taught at Pratt Institute, and for twenty years was head of the Art Department of Manhattanville College.

Mrs. Dowden has both written and illustrated several books for young readers: *Look at a Flower* and *The Secret Life of a Flower* (both botanical studies) and *Roses* (a book of history and legend). With Jessica Kerr, she is responsible for *Shakespeare's Flowers*, which *The New York Times* called "one of the most magnificent treasures to appear in a long time."

56

PRINTED IN BELGIUM BY ⊠